THE
LITTLE BOOK
of
LOVE

ALSO PUBLISHED BY ONEWORLD

The Prophet
Jesus: The Son of Man
Kahlil Gibran: A Spiritual Treasury
Love Letters
Kahlil Gibran, Man & Poet: A New Biography

THE
LITTLE BOOK *of*
LOVE

KAHLIL GIBRAN

Compiled and with an introduction by
Suheil Bushrui

ONEWORLD
OXFORD

THE LITTLE BOOK OF LOVE

First published by Oneworld Publications, 2007
First published in this revised, expanded edition, 2008

ISBN 978–1–85168–627–8

Typeset by Jayvee, Trivandrum, India
Printed and bound in Great Britain by TJ International

Oneworld Publications
185 Banbury Road
Oxford OX2 7AR
England
www.oneworld-publications.com

Dedicated to

MB

My first glimpse of you was not in truth the first. The hour in which our hearts met confirmed in me the belief in Eternity and in the immortality of the Soul.

KAHLIL GIBRAN

INTRODUCTION

'Let love, human and frail, command the coming day' was Kahlil Gibran's call to his generation; a generation that found itself bereft of faith and moral guidance and brutally devastated by the horrors of a savage war. The simplicity and sincerity of his message and his vigorous exaltation of love revived, in many a heart, the eternal values that sustain us as human beings. As time passed, universal renown for his work and warm affection for his character grew beyond anything achieved by any poet of his time.

For millions of his admirers, Gibran's most celebrated work, *The Prophet*, came to be revered as a sacred book, and many 'canonized' him as a new 'prophet' of love. For lovers everywhere, the words of *The Prophet* became a new 'bible', read at marriages and on every occasion lovers wished to solemnise. He continues to inspire generation after generation of the young and idealistic. The Flower Children of the 1960s hailed Gibran as their prophet and declared that love was the new religion. The songs and music of the Flower Children seemed to distil Gibran's message, most notably in one of the most famous songs of the twentieth century, *All You Need Is Love*, written by John Lennon and sung by The Beatles.

Love was the major theme of Kahlil Gibran's work, and his interpretation of the universe was based on his belief that all creation is permeated by love. Love, for Gibran, was both a holistic state of being and a deeply spiritual experience, a 'sacred mystery' that 'remains forever wordless'. It is impossible to define such a love, though it includes spiritual and platonic elements: Gibran leaves us in no doubt that the only path to self-realisation is the path of true love. In other words, everyone is on a pilgrimage towards that celestial city of love eternal.

Gibran's concept of love is not an artificial romantic affectation, but a positive romantic rapture and ecstasy, despite the fact that love can be wounding, painful, and entail great suffering. Gibran found this aspect in the writings of both the eastern Sufis and the mediaeval Christian mystics. The influence of William Blake is also clearly evident in Gibran's insistence on the essential identity of joy, pain and sorrow as major features of his intensely personal concept of love, a concept that rejected the limiting dualism of the material world. By refusing to provide a definition, Gibran allowed us – through the many statements he made about love – to realise that love is many-sided. He also warned against the dangers of falling into hypocrisy and self-deception. Love, according to Gibran, is a serious matter and makes demands on us; it has its own laws, rights and responsibilities, and in its truest form should lead us to a deeper understanding of ourselves.

The selections in this anthology represent an attempt to include the many different aspects of love that Gibran refers to in his works: the love of God; the love of country; the love of family and friends; the love between men and women; the love of nature; and the love of all humanity. It is hoped that these short passages will also demonstrate the sense of compassion Gibran expresses in his view of men and women, who are seen to be equally in need of self-realisation. Only through the knowledge of the heart are we able to achieve self-knowledge: words become powerless and inadequate. The perennial question, which is universally asked, occurs in *The Prophet*: 'Who among you does not feel that his power to love is boundless?'

For Gibran, love remained the supreme virtue and the dynamic force that enhanced the life of the world and the spirit. For him, no gift can ever compare with the unique gift which only love can offer.

KHALIL GIBRAN:
A BIOGRAPHICAL NOTE

Kahlil Gibran (1883–1931) was born near the sacred cedar grove of Bisharri, in the Lebanon. He spent most of his adult life in the west – chiefly the United States – having emigrated from his homeland in 1895 at the age of twelve. His attachment to Lebanon, reinforced by two years at the al-Hikmah (La Sagesse) school in Beirut, between 1898 and 1901, remained strong.

The influences on Gibran as a writer and painter were an equal mixture of Eastern and Western elements. His literary career can be divided into two phases: the Arabic period from 1905 to 1918 and the English period from 1918 to 1931. However, throughout his literary career, the Bible, a book belonging neither to East nor West, remained one of the most profound and enduring influences on his life and thought.

Gibran's early Arabic writings, which established him as the foremost exponent of Romanticism in Arabic literature, are characterised by a strong sense of bitterness and disillusionment. He advocates sweeping reforms, bemoans the injustice meted out to women, directs scathing attacks on all forms of political and religious corruption and cupidity and expresses his rebellion against the strictures and outdated values of a bigoted and feudalistic society. These early works also show signs of the basic themes of his later writings: a spirited defence of women's rights, which later became one of the strongest elements in his thought, and a belief in the healing power of Universal Love and in the Unity of Being – the chief message of his great work *The Prophet* (1923).

The second phase of Gibran's career saw the publication of his eight English language works, including two posthumous works: *The Wanderer* and *The Garden of the Prophet*. *Twenty Drawings* (1919), containing what many believe to be Gibran's finest works of art up to that date, was also published in this period. His paintings and drawings, and to some extent his writings, bear the unmistakable influence of William Blake. Nowhere is Gibran's mystical bent more evident than in *Twenty Drawings*.

His message found ample expression in his English works, especially in *The Prophet*, which shows his view of life through the relation of man to man, and reflects his ideas on topics such as marriage, law, freedom, crime and punishment, generosity, religion, death, pain and pleasure and above all, love. For Gibran, love is the key to all things.

LOVE GIVES naught but itself and takes
   naught but from itself.
Love possesses not nor would it be
   possessed;
For love is sufficient unto love.

When you love you should not say,
   'God is in my heart',
But rather, 'I am in the heart of God'.
And think not you can direct the
   course of love,
For love, if it finds you worthy, directs
   your course.
Love has no other desire but to fulfil itself.

THE PROPHET

WILL YOU accept a heart that loves,
But never yields? And burns, but
Never melts? Will you be at ease
With a soul that quivers before the
Tempest, but never surrenders to it?
Will you accept one as a companion
Who makes not slaves, nor will become
One? Will you own me but not possess
Me, by taking my body and not my heart?

THE SECRETS OF THE HEART

MY SOUL preached to me and taught me to love that which the people abhor and befriend him whom they revile.

My soul showed me that Love prides itself not only in the one who loves, but also in the beloved.

Ere my soul preached to me, Love was in my heart as a tiny thread fastened between two pegs.

But now Love has become a halo whose beginning is its end, and whose end is its beginning. It surrounds every being and extends slowly to embrace all that shall be.

THOUGHTS AND MEDITATIONS

THERE IS no force in this world that can rob me of my happiness, for it springs from the embrace of two souls held together by understanding and sheltered by love.

SPIRITS REBELLIOUS

LOVE KNOWS not its depth till the hour of separation.

SPIRITUAL SAYINGS

LOVE ONE another, but make not a bond of
    love:
Let it rather be a moving sea between the
    shores of your souls.
Fill each other's cup but drink not from
    one cup.
Give one another of your bread but eat not
    from the same loaf.
Sing and dance together and be joyous,
    but let each one of you be alone,
Even as the strings of a lute are alone
    though they quiver with the same music.

Give your hearts, but not into each other's
    keeping.
For only the hand of Life can contain your
    hearts.
And stand together yet not too near
    together:
For the pillars of the temple stand apart,
And the oak tree and the cypress grow not in
    each other's shadow.

THE PROPHET

IN TRUTH have earthly bodies desires
    unbeknown
And must they oft-times separate for
    earthly purpose,
And remain apart for worldly reason.
But all spirits abide in safety in love's hands
Till Death do come and bear them aloft to
    God.

A TEAR AND A SMILE

YOU ARE a slave to him whom you love
        because you love him.
And a slave to him who loves you
        because he loves you.

SAND AND FOAM

LOVE IS the only freedom in the world
        because it so elevates the spirit that the
        laws of humanity and the phenomena of
nature do not alter its course.

THE BROKEN WINGS

WHAT THING is this love? Whence does it come? What does it want of a youth resting with his flock among the ruined shrines? What is this wine which courses through the veins of one whom maidens' glances left unmoved? What are these heavenly melodies that rise and fall upon the ears of a Bedouin who heard not yet the sweet songs of women?

What thing is this love and whence does it come? What does it want of Ali, busied with his sheep and his flute away from men? Is it something sowed in his heart by man-wrought beauties without the awareness of his senses? Or is it a bright light veiled by the mist and now breaking forth to illumine the emptiness of his soul? Is it perchance a dream come in the stillness of the night to mock at him, or a truth that was and will be to the end of time?

NYMPHS OF THE VALLEY

I PURIFIED my lips with the sacred fire to
    speak of love,
But when I opened my lips I found myself
    speechless.
Before I knew love, I was wont to chant
    the songs of love,
But when I learned to know, the words
    in my mouth became naught save breath,
And the tunes within my breast fell into
    deep silence.

PROSE POEMS

A WOMAN'S HAPPINESS is not in the glory and lordship of a man. Neither is it in his generosity or clemency; it is in a love that binds her spirit to his spirit, pouring out her love into his heart and making them a single member in the body of Life and one word on the lips of God.

SPIRITS REBELLIOUS

12 ❧ *Gibran*

THEY SAY the nightingale pierces his bosom
    with a thorn when he sings a love song.
So do we all. How else should we sing?

SAND AND FOAM

LOVE IS a resolution which accompanies
our being, and binds this present with the
ages past and future.

PROSE POEMS

A POET ONCE wrote a love song and it was beautiful. And he made many copies of it, and sent them to his friends and acquaintances, both men and women, and even to a young woman whom he had met once, who lived beyond the mountains.

And in a day or two a messenger came from the young woman bringing a letter. And in the letter she said, "Let me assure you, I am deeply touched by the love song that you have written to me. Come now, and see my father and my mother, and we shall make arrangements for the betrothal."

And the poet answered the letter, and he said to her, "My friend, it was but a song of love out of a poet's heart, sung by every man to every woman."

And she wrote again to him saying, "Hypocrite and liar in words! From this day unto my coffin-day I shall hate all poets for your sake."

THE WANDERER

LET LOVE, human and frail, command the
coming day.

THE EARTH GODS

WAS THE love of Judas' mother for her
son less than the love of Mary for
Jesus?

SAND AND FOAM

LOVE IS a celestial light shining from the
    innermost of the sensitive self to illumine
    all about it,
That it may behold the world as a procession
    moving in green meadows,
And life as a dream of beauty between
    awakening and awakening.

PROSE POEMS

LIFE WITHOUT Love is like a tree without blossom and fruit. And Love without Beauty is like flowers without scent and fruits without seeds … Life, Love, and Beauty are three persons in one, who cannot be separated or changed.

THOUGHTS AND MEDITATIONS

I YEARN TOWARD my land for its beauty; and I love those that dwell thereon for their weariness.

But did my people take up the sword, saying it was out of love of their land, and fall upon my neighbour's land and plunder its goods and slay its men and render its children orphans and make its women widows, and water its soil with its sons' blood and feed to the prowling beast the flesh of its youth, I would hate my land and its people ...

I love the place of my birth with some of the love for my land;

I love my country with a little of my love for the world, my homeland;

I love the world with my all, for it is the pastureland of Man, the spirit of divinity on earth.

A TEAR AND A SMILE

Those whom Love has not chosen as
followers do not hear when Love calls.

THE BROKEN WINGS

LOVE IS a distant laughter in the spirit.
It is a wild assault that hushes you to your
    awakening.
It is a new dawn unto the earth,
A day not yet achieved in your eyes or mine,
But already achieved in its own greater heart.

THE EARTH GODS

LOVE IS a dense fog to enshroud the soul,
    and veil from it the shows of life,
So that the soul sees naught but the
    shadows of its desires
Lost among rocky steeps,
And hears naught but the echo of its voice
    shouting from the valleys of desolation.

PROSE POEMS

LOVE THAT comes between the *naïveté* and awakening of youth satisfies itself with possessing, and grows with embraces. But Love which is born in the firmament's lap and has descended with the night's secrets is not contented with anything but Eternity and immortality; it does not stand reverently before anything except deity.

THE BROKEN WINGS

L OVE THAT does not renew itself every day becomes a habit and in turn a slavery.

SAND AND FOAM

WHEN LOVE beckons to you, follow him,
Though his ways are hard and steep.
And when his wings enfold you yield to him,
Though the sword hidden among his
    pinions may wound you.
And when he speaks to you believe in him,
Though his voice may shatter your dreams
    as the North Wind lays waste the garden.
For even as love crowns you so shall he
    crucify you. Even as he is for your growth
    so is he for your pruning.
Even as he ascends to your height and
    caresses your tenderest branches that
    quiver in the sun,
So shall he descend to your roots and shake
    them in their clinging to the earth.
Like sheaves of corn he gathers you unto
    himself.
He threshes you to make you naked.
He sifts you to free you from your husks.
He grinds you to whiteness.
He kneads you until you are pliant;

And then he assigns you to his sacred fire,
that you may become sacred bread for
God's sacred feast.

THE PROPHET

How shall my heart be unsealed unless it be broken?

SAND AND FOAM

Love is a heavenly wisdom that lights our inner and outer eye so that we may behold all things even as the gods.

PROSE POEMS

I know not what to say, My Beloved, but my soul will pour itself into parchment … my soul that suffers through separation, but is consoled by Love that renders pain a joy, and sorrow a happiness. When Love unified our hearts, and we looked to the day when our two hearts would be joined by the mighty breath of God …

BETWEEN NIGHT AND MORN

OF ALL people you are the nearest to my soul, and the nearest to my heart, and our souls and hearts have never quarrelled. Only our thoughts have quarrelled, and thought is acquired, it is derived from the environment, from what we see in front of us, from what each day brings to us; but soul and heart formed a sublime essence in us long before our thoughts. The function of thought is to organize and arrange, and this is a good function and necessary for our social lives, but it has no place in the life of the heart and soul. 'If we should quarrel hereafter we must not go our separate ways'. Thought can say this despite being the cause of all quarrelling, but it cannot utter one word about love, nor is it able to measure the soul in terms of words, nor to weigh the heart in the scales of its logic.

LETTER TO MAY ZIADEH

NOW SHOULD you meet a lover lost,
    Bewildered, yet avoiding guide,
Disdaining though he thirsts to drink,
    In his own hunger satisfied.

Hear people say, 'This youth bewitched
    'What seek he from a love so great?
'What hope has he to patiently
    'Await his Kismet and his Fate?

'Why waste his bloodstained tears for one
    'Who lacks all beauty and respect?'
Say of them all, they are stillborn,
    Know naught of life, nor can reflect.

THE PROCESSION

LOVE IS a sacred mystery.
To those who love, it remains forever wordless;
But to those who do not love, it may be but a
heartless jest.

JESUS, THE SON OF MAN

BE SILENT, my heart, until Dawn comes,
For he who patiently awaits the morn
Will meet him surely, and he who loves
The light will be loved by the light.

BETWEEN NIGHT AND MORN

It is but the love of a blind man who knows not the beauty of one nor the ugliness of another.

THE FORERUNNER

For love when love is homesick exhausts time's measurements and time's soundings.

THE GARDEN OF THE PROPHET

MY HEART was weary within me and bade me farewell and repaired to the Abode of Happiness. And when it was come to that sanctuary which the spirit had sanctified, it stood in wonderment, for it saw not there things it had imagined.

It saw not there power or wealth, nor yet authority. It saw naught save the youth of Beauty and his companion the daughter of Love and their child Wisdom.

Then my heart spoke to the daughter of Love and said: 'Where is contentment, O Love? I had heard that it shared with you this dwelling.' And she answered: 'Contentment is away preaching in the city, where is corruption and greed; we are not in need of it in this place. Happiness desires not contentment, for happiness is naught but a longing which union embraces; contentment is a diversion conquered by forgetfulness. The immortal soul is not contented, for it is ever desiring of perfection; and perfection is the Infinite.'

And my heart spoke to the youth of Beauty and said: 'Show to me the secret of woman, O Beauty, and enlighten me, for you are knowledge.' He said: 'She is you, human heart, and as you were, so was she. She is I, and wheresoever I be, there is she. She is as a religion when the ignorant profane it not; as a full moon when clouds do not hide it; as the breeze untouched by corruption and impurity.'

Then my heart drew near to Wisdom, the daughter of Love and Beauty, saying: 'Give me wisdom that I may carry it to humankind.' She answered: 'Say that happiness begins in the holy of holies of the spirit and comes not from without.'

A Tear and a Smile

I WALK SIDE by side with a shadow more beautiful and more lucid than the reality of all men. I walk [with my hand] holding a hand that is silken and yet strong, with a will of its own; a hand whose fingers are soft and yet capable of lifting weights and breaking heavy chains. And every now and then I turn my head to behold a pair of glittering eyes and lips touched by a smile that wounds with its sweetness.

LETTER TO MAY ZIADEH

I KNOW THAT the silence of the night is the worthiest messenger between our two hearts, for she bears Love's message and recites the psalms of our hearts. Just as God has made our souls prisoners of our bodies, so Love has made me a prisoner of words and speech.

THE VOICE OF THE MASTER

IT IS wrong to think that love comes from long companionship and persevering courtship. Love is the offspring of spiritual affinity and unless that affinity is created in a moment, it will not be created in years or even generations.

THE BROKEN WINGS

LOVE IS a nectar which the brides of dawn
    pour for the strong
So that they rise glorified before the
    stars of night, and joyous before the
    sun of day.

PROSE POEMS

YOUR NEIGHBOUR is your other self
      dwelling behind a wall.
In understanding, all walls shall fall down.
Who knows but that your neighbour is
      your better self wearing another
      body? See that you love him as you
      would love yourself.

JESUS, THE SON OF MAN

LOVE AND doubt have never been on
    speaking terms.

SAND AND FOAM

HE PERCEIVED the feathery touch of delicate wings rustling about his flaming heart, and a great love possessing him … A love whose power separates the mind from the world of quantity and measurement … A love that talks when the tongue of Life is muted … A love that stands as a blue beacon to point out the path, guiding with no visible light.

BETWEEN NIGHT AND MORN

LOVE IS youth with chains broken,
Manhood made free from the sod,
And womanhood warmed by the flame
And shining with the light of heaven
    deeper than our heaven.

THE EARTH GODS

LOVE IS gracious host to his guests though
to the unbidden his house is a mirage and
a mockery.

JESUS, THE SON OF MAN

LOVE TRIUMPHS.

The white and green of love beside a lake,
And the proud majesty of love in tower or balcony;
Love in a garden or in the desert untrodden,
Love is our lord and master.
It is not a wanton decay of the flesh,
Nor the crumbling of desire
When desire and self are wrestling;
Nor is it flesh that takes arms against the spirit.
Love rebels not.
It only leaves the trodden way of ancient
    destinies for the sacred grove,
To sing and dance its secret to eternity.

THE EARTH GODS

A MAN AND a woman sat by a window that opened upon Spring. They sat close one unto the other. And the woman said, "I love you. You are handsome, and you are rich, and you are always well-attired."

And the man said, "I love you. You are a beautiful thought, a thing too apart to hold in the hand, and a song in my dreaming."

But the woman turned from him in anger, and she said, "Sir, please leave me now. I am not a thought, and I am not a thing that passes in your dreams. I am a woman. I would have you desire me, a wife, and the mother of unborn children."

And they parted.

And the man was saying in his heart, "Behold another dream is even now turned into the mist."

And the woman was saying, "Well, what of a man who turns me into a mist and a dream?"

THE WANDERER

NIGHT IS over, and we children of night must die when dawn comes leaping upon the hills; and out of our ashes a mightier love shall rise. And it shall laugh in the sun, and it shall be deathless.

THE FORERUNNER

WORK IS love made visible.

THE PROPHET

ALL LIFE is twain, the one a frozen stream,
   the other a burning flame,
And the burning flame is love.

PROSE POEMS

EVEN THE wisest among us bows under the
heavy weight of Love; but in truth she is
as light as the frolicsome breeze of
Lebanon.

THE VOICE OF THE MASTER

I AND the shore are lovers:
The wind unites us and separates us.

I come from beyond the twilight
To merge the silver of my foam with
    the gold of its sand;
And I cool its burning heart with my
    moisture.

At dawn's coming I read passion's
    law to my beloved,
And he draws me to his breast.
At even I chant the prayer of longing,
And he embraces me.

A TEAR AND A SMILE

IN THE woods no blame attaches
    To lovers' tryst, nor watchers spy;
When a gazelle, ranging swiftly,
    Greets its lovemate with a cry,

Eagles never display wonder,
    Or say, ' 'Tis a marvel of the age'.
For in nature we the children
    Only hold the sane as strange.

THE PROCESSION

... HER BODY trembled like the trembling of a lily before the breeze of daybreak. The light in her heart overflowed from her eyes, and shyness fought with her tongue for mastery, and she said: 'We are both of us between the hands of a hidden force, a just and merciful force; let it do with us as it will.'

SPIRITS REBELLIOUS

O LOVE, whose lordly hand
Has bridled my desires,
And raised my hunger and my thirst
To dignity and pride,
Let not the strong in me and the constant
Eat the bread or drink the wine
That tempt my weaker self.
Let me rather starve,
And let my heart parch with thirst,
And let me die and perish,
Ere I stretch my hand
To a cup you did not fill,
Or a bowl you did not bless.

THE FORERUNNER

YESTERDAY I stood at the temple door interrogating the passers-by about the mystery and merit of Love.

And before me passed an old man with an emaciated and melancholy face, who sighed and said:

'Love is a natural weakness bestowed upon us by the first man.'

But a virile youth retorted:

'Love joins our present with the past and the future.'

Then a woman with a tragic face sighed and said:

'Love is a deadly poison injected by black vipers, that crawl from the caves of hell. The poison seems fresh as dew and the thirsty soul eagerly drinks it; but after the first intoxication the drinker sickens and dies a slow death.'

Then a beautiful, rosy-cheeked damsel smilingly said:

'Love is a wine served by the brides of Dawn which strengthens strong souls and enables them to ascend to the stars.'

After her a black-robed, bearded man, frowning, said:

'Love is the blind ignorance with which youth begins and ends.'

Another, smiling, declared:

'Love is a divine knowledge that enables men to see as much as the gods.'

'Then said a blind man, feeling his way with a cane:

'Love is a blinding mist that keeps the soul from discerning the secret of existence, so that the heart sees only trembling phantoms of desire among the hills, and hears only echoes of cries from voiceless valleys.'

A young man, playing on his viol, sang:

'Love is a magic ray emitted from the burning core of the soul and illuminating the surrounding earth. It enables us to perceive Life as a beautiful dream between one awakening and another.'

And a feeble ancient, dragging his feet like two rags, said, in quavering tones:

'Love is the rest of the body in the quiet of the grave, the tranquility of the soul in the depth of Eternity.'

And a five-year-old child, after him, said laughing:

'Love is my father and mother, and no one knows Love save my father and mother.'

And so, all who passed spoke of Love as the image of their hopes and frustrations, leaving it a mystery as before.

Then I heard a voice within the temple:

'Life is divided into two halves, one frozen, the other aflame; the burning half is Love.'

THOUGHTS AND MEDITATIONS

I LOVE MY little one, but I do not know in my mind why I love her. I do not want to know in my mind, it is sufficient that I love her. It is sufficient that I love her in my soul and in my heart. It is sufficient for me to rest my head on her shoulder when I am sad, lonely and in solitude, or when I am happy, entranced and full of wonder. It is sufficient for me to walk by her side to the top of the mountain and to tell her every now and then: 'You are my companion, you are my companion'.

LETTER TO MAY ZIADEH

YOU ARE my brother and I love you.
I love you when you prostrate yourself in
    your mosque, and kneel in your
    church, and pray in your synagogue.
You and I are sons of one faith, the Spirit.

A TEAR AND A SMILE

LOVE COMES in different shapes. Sometimes
    it comes in wisdom; at other times in
    justice; and oftentimes in hope.

THOUGHTS AND MEDITATIONS

TELL ME, for Love's sake, what is that flame which burns in my heart and devours my strength and dissolves my will?

THOUGHTS AND MEDITATIONS

THE FIRST glance from the eyes of the beloved is like the spirit that moved upon the face of the waters, giving birth to heaven and earth, when the Lord spoke and said, 'Let there be.'

THE VOICE OF THE MASTER

LOVE IS a word of light, written by a hand of
light, upon a page of light.

SAND AND FOAM

THERE IS no punishment so severe as that
suffered by the woman who finds herself
imprisoned between a man she loves and
another man who loves her.

THE SECRETS OF THE HEART

…WITH MY lips I have denounced you, while my heart, bleeding within me, called you tender names.

THE FORERUNNER

WHEN LOVE becomes vast love becomes wordless.

JESUS, THE SON OF MAN

M Y FIRST glimpse of you was not in truth the first. The hour in which our hearts met confirmed in me the belief in Eternity and in the immortality of the Soul.

THE VOICE OF THE MASTER

L OVE PASSES us by, robed in meekness; but we flee from her in fear, or hide in the darkness; or else pursue her, to do evil in her name.

THE VOICE OF THE MASTER

A WOMAN SAID unto a man, 'I love you'. And the man said, 'It is in my heart to be worthy of your love.'

And the woman said, 'You love me not?'

And the man only gazed upon her and said nothing.

Then the woman cried aloud, 'I hate you'. And the man said 'Then it is also in my heart to be worthy of your hate.'

THE WANDERER

THEN HE looked at me, and the noontide of His eyes was upon me, and He said: 'You have many lovers, and yet I alone love you. Other men love themselves in your nearness. I love you in your self. Other men see a beauty in you that shall fade away sooner than their own years. But I see in you a beauty that shall not fade away, and in the autumn of your days that beauty shall not be afraid to gaze at itself in the mirror, and it shall not be offended.

'I alone love the unseen in you.'

JESUS, THE SON OF MAN

LOVE, LIKE death, changes everything.

SPIRITUAL SAYINGS

LOVERS EMBRACE that which is between them rather than each other.

SAND AND FOAM

YOU HAVE the great gift of understanding, beloved Mary. You are a life-giver, Mary. You are like the Great Spirit, who befriends man not only to share his life, but to add to it. My knowing you is the greatest thing in my days and nights, a miracle quite outside the natural order of things.

I have always held, with my *Madman*, that those who understand us enslave something in us. It is not so with you. Your understanding of me is the most peaceful freedom I have known. And in the last two hours of your last visit you took my heart in your hand and found a black spot in it. But just as soon as you found the spot it was erased forever, and I became absolutely chainless.

LETTER TO MARY HASKELL

FOR LOVE lies in the soul alone,
    Not in the body, and like wine
Should stimulate our better self
    To welcome gifts of Love Divine.

THE PROCESSION

LOVE IS a force that makes our hearts; our hearts cannot create that force.

SPIRITS REBELLIOUS

HERE I sit between my brother the mountain and my sister the sea.

We three are one in loneliness, and the love that binds us together is deep and strong and strange. Nay, it is deeper than my sister's depth and stronger than my brother's strength, and stranger than the strangeness of my madness.

Aeons upon aeons have passed since the first grey dawn made us visible to one another; and though we have seen the birth and the fulness and the death of many worlds, we are still eager and young.

We are young and eager and yet we are mateless and unvisited, and though we lie in unbroken half embrace, we are uncomforted. And what comfort is there for controlled desire and unspent passion? Whence shall come the flaming god to warm my sister's bed? And what she-torrent shall quench my brother's fire? And who is the woman that shall command my heart?

In the stillness of the night my sister murmurs in her sleep the fire-god's unknown name, and my brother calls afar upon the cool and distant goddess. But upon whom I call in my sleep I know not.

Here I sit between my brother the mountain
and my sister the sea. We three are one in
loneliness, and the love that binds us together
is deep and strong and strange.

THE MADMAN

As the first glance from the eyes of the beloved is like a seed sown in the human heart, and the first kiss of her lips like a flower upon the branch of the Tree of Life, so the union of two lovers in marriage is like the first fruit of the first flower of that seed.

THE VOICE OF THE MASTER

THE TWO lovers walked among the willow trees, and the oneness of each was a language speaking of the oneness of both; and an ear listening in silence to the inspiration of love; and a seeing eye seeing the glory of happiness.

NYMPHS OF THE VALLEY

YOU TELL me that you fear love; why, my little one? Do you fear the light of the sun? Do you fear the ebb and flow of the sea? Do you fear the dawning of the day? Do you fear the advent of spring? I wonder why you fear love? ... do not fear love; do not fear love, friend of my heart. We must surrender to it in spite of what it may bring in the way of pain, of desolation, of longing, and in spite of all perplexity and bewilderment.

LETTER TO MAY ZIADEH

DRY YOUR tears, my darling, for love that has opened our eyes and made us its servants will grant us the blessing of patience and forbearance. Dry your tears and be consoled, for we have made a covenant with love, and for that love shall we bear the torment of poverty and the bitterness of misfortune and the pain of separation.

A TEAR AND A SMILE

LOVE IS an inborn weakness which we have inherited from the first man.

PROSE POEMS

BUT LOVE is beyond our questioning,
And love outsoars our song.

THE EARTH GODS

ACKNOWLEDGEMENTS

In the preparation of this volume, I have received much valuable help and guidance from Ms Juliet Mabey, and especially from my assistant, Miss Poupak Moallem, who took the responsibility of preparing the final text for press.

Acknowledgement is hereby extended to Alfred A. Knopf, a division of Random House, Inc., for permission to reprint material from *The Prophet* by Kahlil Gibran, copyright 1923 by Kahlil Gibran and renewed 1951 by Administrators C. T. A. of Kahlil Gibran Estate and Mary G. Gibran. Acknowledgement is also extended to the following publishers and holders of copyright: the Administrators C. T. A. of Kahlil Gibran Estate and Mary G. Gibran for permission to reprint material from the following books by Kahlil Gibran: *The Madman, The Forerunner, Sand and Foam, Jesus, the Son of Man, The Earth Gods, The Wanderer, The Garden of the Prophet, A Tear and a Smile, Nymphs of the Valley, Beloved Prophet, Prose Poems*; Anthony R. Ferris for extracts from

Spiritual Sayings, Thoughts and Meditations; S. B. Bushrui and Salma Haffar al-Kuzbari for extracts from *Love Letters*; The Citadel Press for extracts from *The Broken Wings*, *Secrets of the Heart*, *The Voice of the Master*; Mrs G. Kheirallah for extracts from *The Procession*; Philosophical Library, Inc. for extracts from *Between Night and Morn*, copyright 1965.